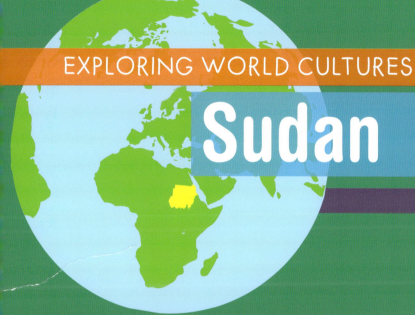

Exploring World Cultures

Sudan

By Corina Jeffries

Cavendish
Square

New York

Published in 2022 by Cavendish Square Publishing, LLC
29 East 21st Street New York, NY 10010

Library of Congress Cataloging-in-Publication Data

Names: Jeffries, Corina, author.
Title: Sudan / Corina Jeffries.
Other titles: Exploring world cultures.
Description: First edition. | New York : Cavendish Square Publishing,
[2022] | Series: Exploring world cultures | Includes bibliographical
references and index.
Identifiers: LCCN 2020039632 | ISBN 9781502662514 (library binding) | ISBN
9781502662491 (paperback) | ISBN 9781502662507 (set) | ISBN
9781502662521 (ebook)
Subjects: LCSH: Sudan--Juvenile literature.
Classification: LCC DT154.6 .J44 2022 | DDC 962.4--dc23
LC record available at https://lccn.loc.gov/2020039632

Editor: Caitie McAneney
Copyeditor: Jill Keppeler
Designer: Rachel Rising

CPSIA compliance information: Batch #CW22CSQ: For further information contact Cavendish Square Publishing LLC, New York, New York, at 1-877-980-4450.

Printed in the United States of America

Find us on

Contents

Sudan is a **diverse** country. It's home to many different groups of people, as well as wildlife and landscapes. Many people have moved into and through this African country throughout

Khartoum is the capital of Sudan. It's where the White and Blue Nile Rivers meet.

history. It has been a crossroads between areas around the Mediterranean Sea and the rest of Africa. People brought their religions, languages, and customs to the area.

Sudan has more pyramids than any other country! Parts of Sudan and Egypt once made up the ancient **region** of Nubia. Many empires

Sudan has many important customs, or practices.

and nations have ruled this region, each making their mark on it.

Today, the country of Sudan has both small settlements and city centers. Most people live along waterways, including the Nile River system and its tributaries, or offshoots. People in Sudan face many challenges, including **conflicts**, dry weather, and **poverty**. However, they also have many special customs and diverse cultures, or ways of life.

Sudan is a country of wide, dry spaces and life-giving rivers. It's in Northern Africa, a part of Africa affected by Arab culture. Egypt is to the north, and South Sudan is to the south. Chad, Libya, and the Central African Republic are to the west. Ethiopia and Eritrea are to the east, as is the Red Sea.

Strong dust storms called haboobs can happen in central Sudan.

The northern half of Sudan is part of the Sahara, the largest hot desert in the world. Most

South Sudan was part of Sudan until 2011.

Deserts are areas with very little rainfall. Sudan's deserts are sandy or rocky. Few or no plants grow there.

of the country has plains or plateaus, which are large, raised areas. Hills and mountains in Sudan include the Red Sea Hills in the northeast, the Nuba Mountains (or Nuba Hills) in the south, and the Marrah Mountains in the west.

The Sahel is an area between the Sahara and Africa's savannas, or grasslands.

Rivers are very important to people in Sudan. The Nile River system provides water to the land and its peoples.

Ancient Nubia was the area that's now northern Sudan and southern Egypt. The area was a crossroads of trade between European Mediterranean countries, regions in the Arabian Desert, and African countries.

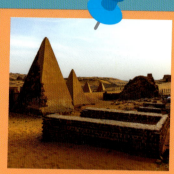

Kushites built many grand pyramids for their kings and queens.

Later, the kingdom of Kush rose to power in the region and took over ancient Egypt for a time. The Kushites later made Meroë, along Sudan's part of the Nile River, their capital.

FACT!

Child soldiers have been forced to fight in conflicts around the world, including in Sudan.

Civil War

The Second Sudanese Civil War (1983-2005) killed and **displaced** millions. Muslim Arabs in northern Sudan fought against southerners of different religions.

After Kush, smaller kingdoms ruled different parts of Sudan. Christians spread their religion,

Around 20,000 children, called the "Lost Boys," fled Sudan during the second civil war.

or belief system, in the sixth century AD. Arabs spread Islam in the seventh century. Different kingdoms followed different faiths.

Egypt took over northern Sudan in 1820. It was under British-Egyptian rule for a time. Sudan became independent in 1956. Bloody civil wars, or fighting within the country, followed independence.

9

VOTE ✓

Sudan has seen many changes in its government after independence. There have been uprisings and shifts in power. Sudan's

Sudanese protesters gather in Khartoum in 2019.

constitution, or set of laws, has also changed. Conflicts have stemmed from Islamist leaders ruling under **fundamentalist** laws called sharia.

The civil wars in Sudan ended with an agreement in 2005. The agreement included the creation of South Sudan, which became an independent country in 2011. The governments of

FACT!

Sudan is divided into 18 states, or *wilayat*.

both Sudan and South Sudan are still unstable.

In 2019, long-time **authoritarian** president Omar al-Bashir was overthrown. Now, Sudan is in a state of change. Many people want a democracy. Democracy would give a

Women such as Alaa Salah led protests against al-Bashir in 2019.

voice to the people. Many other Arab countries demanded democracy during a period of protests beginning in late 2010 called the Arab Spring.

Darfur

Darfur is in western Sudan. Sudan's government started a **genocide** in Darfur in 2003, killing and displacing millions of people. Many **refugees** fled to other countries.

The Economy

Sudan's economy— its system of making, buying, and selling goods and services— is affected by its government and natural surroundings. Many

Sudanese farmers often use water from the Nile to irrigate, or water, their crops.

people take part in subsistence farming. That means they grow food and raise livestock just for their families or close communities.

Some parts of Sudan are good for raising cattle. Farmers also grow cotton, groundnuts

The main unit of money in Sudan is the Sudanese pound.

Striking Oil

In 1977, people found oil in Sudan. It became an important export. However, much of this oil is now found in today's South Sudan and not in Sudan.

(peanuts), sweet potatoes, millet, and sugarcane. They grow tropical fruits such as papayas, mangoes, and bananas. One important **resource** is gum arabic, which is sap from one kind of tree. It's used to make medicines, inks, paints, and food.

Sudan exports some of its goods, or sells them to other countries. It exports oil, cotton, livestock, and gum arabic.

Livestock animals in Sudan include cattle, sheep, goats, and camels.

Southern areas of Sudan are tropical, or warm with rainy seasons. Northern areas are hot and dry. Temperatures regularly reach above 100 degrees Fahrenheit (37.8 degrees Celsius).

Some animals are kept safe in parks in Sudan.

The savanna is home to many big animals such as giraffes and elephants. Predators include lions, leopards, and cheetahs. Plant life depends on the region. Savannas have many grasses and trees, while deserts support few plants.

FACT!

Climate change leads to floods in some places and droughts, or dry periods, in other places.

Food and Water

Some people suffer a lack of food and water in Sudan. If there's not enough water, people can't grow food for their families.

The environment, or natural world, in Sudan faces many challenges. Many animals have lost their natural environments or

Animals, plants, and people suffer when there's not enough water.

have been killed by hunters. The desert grows bigger each year, taking over rich soil. Erosion, or the wearing down of soil, makes it hard for plants to grow. Hot, dry weather leads to harmful grass fires. Dust storms can bury homes under sand. Climate change may force people from their homes in Sudan.

Around 45.5 million people live in Sudan today. Because many older people died in conflicts and the civil wars, much of the population is very young.

Nomads travel to new places during the dry season in Sudan.

Many different **ethnic** groups live in Sudan. Many people in the north identify as Sudanese Arabs. These are Muslims who speak Arabic. This shows the effect of Arab movement from

FACT!

Around 42 percent of the population of Sudan is 14 years old or younger.

Nomads

Nomads are people who move from place to place. Several nomadic groups live in Sudan, including the Bedouin (or Bedu). Bedouin live in the desert.

Many groups live in the Nuba Hills of Sudan.

the Middle East to and through Sudan. About 70 percent of the population is Sudanese Arab, but there are many ethnic groups within this larger group.

Non-Arab ethnic groups, including the Fur and Nuba, often speak local languages. The Fur are Muslim Africans living in western Sudan. The Nuba are mainly farmers who live in the Nuba Hills of south-central Sudan. Each larger group has many more groups within it.

Lifestyle

There are many ways of life in Sudan. Different peoples have different homes, customs, families, and ways of getting around.

Women face unfair laws and treatment in Sudan. However, they became leaders during the 2019 protests.

People in Khartoum live a city lifestyle. People travel by rail, boat, or plane to and from Khartoum. People can practice their religion in cathedrals, or grand churches, and **mosques**. Some people in Khartoum are students at colleges such as the University of Khartoum,

FACT!

Honor, respect, politeness, and giving to others are important values in Sudan.

Community and Family

Community and family are very important in Sudan. Families are often large. People help out their community whenever they can.

Homes in Sudan are often made of natural matter, like sun-dried mud bricks and plants.

Nilayn University, or the Sudan University of Science and Technology.

People in rural parts of Sudan live a very different life. Many are farmers who grow crops or raise livestock. They live in smaller villages along waterways or they move around. Some rural areas lack real roads for getting around. Some people in rural areas struggle to find enough resources for their families.

Much of Sudan and South Sudan's conflict stemmed from religion. Northern Sudan mostly follows Islam, while Christians mainly live in South Sudan. People

Muslims gather to pray at this mosque.

who follow Islam are called Muslims.

Islam has been around since the seventh century AD. Muslims believe an angel named Gabriel revealed the words of Allah (God) to the **Prophet** Muhammad. Their main holy text is the Quran.

FACT!

About 97 percent of Sudanese people are Muslim.

20

Islam and Islamists

Not all Muslims are Islamist. An Islamist is someone who supports fundamentalist laws. Islam is faith-based. Islamism is political and **militant**.

Sudanese Muslim women often cover their hair.

People who follow different branches of Islam practice in different ways. Most Muslims in Sudan follow the Sunni branch. Muslim groups are powerful in social groups and government in Sudan. Islamists have been leaders in Sudan since its independence.

A much smaller portion of Sudan is Christian or animist. Animists believe in spirits that affect the lives of humans. Christians follow the teachings of Jesus Christ.

Language

Most people in Sudan speak Arabic. That's the language most used in government and trade, along with English. Arabic is also spoken in other

These girls are reading from the Quran.

MENA (Middle East and North Africa) countries. It's the language of Islam. The Quran is in Arabic.

Many other native languages are spoken in Sudan. Different ethnic groups have their own languages. For example, the nomadic Beja people—who live in Egypt, Sudan, and Eritrea—

People read Arabic from right to left instead of left to right.

speak Bedawi. Many Nubian languages are spoken in different places in Sudan. The Fur and Zaghawa languages are spoken in the southwest and west.

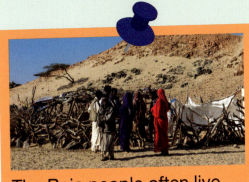

The Beja people often live around the Red Sea.

How do people talk to one another when there are so many different languages? Most people in Sudan are multilingual. That means they speak multiple languages, often including Arabic or English.

Losing Languages

Some languages in Sudan are only spoken by small groups. These peoples sometimes switch to a larger language group like Arabic. Smaller languages are at risk of dying out.

Styles of art and music differ across places and cultural groups in Sudan. In the Blue Nile region, people play a long wind instrument called the *wazza* (sometimes spelled *waza*). These and

Sudanese men play the wazza trumpet.

other instruments are played at weddings and other celebrations, or gatherings. Sudanese artists make pottery and paintings. Storytelling and poetry also are very important parts of Sudanese culture.

FACT!

Oral storytelling, or word-of-mouth storytelling, is an important art form in Sudan.

24

Art as Activism

The authoritarian government of Sudan fell in 2019 after huge protests. Artists used graffiti, or street art, to honor protesters and continue the fight for democracy.

Festivals and celebrations in Sudan are often based around Muslim holy days. The birthday of Muhammad is called

This street art is about the 2019 protests.

Mawlid an-Nabi. People celebrate with singing, dancing, and parties. The end of the Muslim holy month of Ramadan is called Eid al-Fitr. People celebrate in mosques and then gather for meals and gift giving. The Holiya festival in October is a music and dance festival that celebrates a form of Islam called Sufism.

People in Sudan love to play and watch soccer. In Sudan, as in much of the world, it's called football. All you need to play football are two nets and a ball, so the sport is fun for people everywhere.

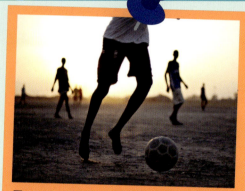

Football is popular, in part, because it can be played anywhere.

Sudan helped found the African Football Confederation in 1957. It won many football competitions in those early years and even won the African Cup of Nations in 1970. The Khartoum

FACT!

Track-and-field events include competitions that involve running, jumping, and throwing.

A Story of Hope

Lopez Lomong was one of the Lost Boys of Sudan. During the civil war, he ran for his life. He then became an Olympic runner for Team USA.

Lopez Lomong is a world-class track star from Sudan.

League is considered the oldest football league, or sports group, in Africa. A number of football clubs play in Sudan. The biggest ones are Al Hilal and Al Merrikh.

Sudanese track-and-field stars are some of the fastest in the world. Many runners compete in the Olympic Games. In 2008, Sudanese runner Ismail Ahmed Ismail won a silver medal at the Olympic games in Beijing, China.

Sudanese people make a kind of bread called *kisra*. It's a spongelike flatbread. It can be used to scoop up foods or dip into stews. A traditional meat and

Food brings people together in Sudan.

vegetable stew in Sudan is called *mullah*. People add spices and peanut butter to stews and other dishes for extra taste. *Ful medames* is a breakfast dish made with fava beans and spices. Usually, hard-boiled eggs or kisra are served with this dish. For dessert, people in Sudan might eat cookies

FACT!

Ful medames is the national dish of Sudan.

28

Drinks in Sudan

In Sudan, people often drink juices made of native fruits. These fruits include *tabaldi* (from the baobab tree), *aradaib* (tamarind), and a kind of berry called *guddaim*.

with dates inside of them.

People in Sudan are resourceful when it comes to food. That means they use what they have. Even though the Sudanese have faced many challenges, their diversity and resourcefulness are part of who they are.

Iftar is a nightly meal in which people gather together after fasting during the Muslim holy month of Ramadan.

Glossary

authoritarian	Concentrating power in a leader not lawfully responsible to the people.
climate change	Change in Earth's weather caused by human activity.
conflict	A fight, battle, or war.
displace	To force people to leave the area where they live.
diverse	Different or varied.
ethnic	Of or relating to large groups of people who have the same cultural background and ways of life.
fundamentalist	A movement or attitude that supports strict following of certain rules or principles.
genocide	The systematic killing of a particular ethnic group.
militant	Using force to support a cause or belief.
mosque	A building used for Muslim religious services.
poverty	The state of being poor.
prophet	Someone who delivers messages that are believed to have come from God.
refugee	Someone who has to leave their home country because it is not safe to stay there.
region	A large area of land that has a number of features in common.
resource	Something that can be used.

Find Out More

Books

Humphreys, Jessica Dee. *Child Soldier: When Boys and Girls Are Used in War*. Toronto, ON: Kids Can Press, 2020.

Rector, Rebecca Kraft. *The Sahara Desert*. Lake Elmo, MN: Focus Readers, 2018.

Website

Sudan
www.ducksters.com/geography/country.php?country=Sudan
Learn more about the geography and peoples of Sudan.

Video

Inside the Burial Chambers of Sudan's Royal Pyramids
www.youtube.com/watch?v=JUl41Oj3tSQ
Explore the Royal Tombs of Nuri with *National Geographic*!

Index

About the Author

Corina Jeffries is a writer and editor from New York. She is passionate about ice cream, libraries, and social justice.